COSMOS.

A Poem.

HENRY S. KING & CO., 65, CORNHILL,
AND 12, PATERNOSTER ROW, LONDON.
1873.

Dedicated,

WITHOUT PERMISSION,

TO

MR. GOLDWIN SMITH.

THE SUBJECT.

MAN AND NATURE.—NATURE IN THE PAST AND IN THE PRESENT.—MAN IN THE PAST AND IN THE PRESENT.—THE FUTURE.

COSMOS.

Hail ! Poet yet unborn, who to your age
Would shew the working heart of ours laid bare,
The wars in which our warriors engage,
The conquests, first our pride, and then our care.
You—or whether an epic tale you tell
Of our long siege of nature, from whose cell
The secret of our ravished race is sought
That knowledge may our rescue bring about;
Or holding mirror to the world of thought
You dramatize it with our human will,
And bear the travail of our weary doubt
Big with a fate it cannot yet fulfil ;
Or, brooding o'er our life, you vivify

8 *Cosmos.*

Its actions, passions, with a lyric cry,

Its little manners, large machinery—

Must subject to your song our conquests won,

Our lights and cross-lights drawn from every sun,

Our triumphs that link time from van to rear,

That sweep through space as their own thoroughfare,

Making the unseen as a ghost appear

And whisper secrets from beyond our sphere,

That, stopping still at death, are everywhere

Within the subtlest, finest-reasoned air;

Conquests that ever grew, that you will find

Affect your own more even than our mind,

Become the common thought-food of mankind.

Lost in the landscape, man's thought first appeared

Viewing its varied presence as his lord,

The sun or earth, what most he liked or feared

Seemed to him living gods to be adored,

Himself the sport of gods loved or abhorred ;

Cosmos. 9

Then, his soul found, its life had life alone,

Mere bounties were but for its welfare grown,

The lights of heaven for its enlargement shone;

Now, nature, as the state in which man lives,

By whose sure laws alone he works and thrives,

Receives interpretation and then gives,

And we, far from the wave-washed landmarks past,

Doubt that there is a land that can be trod,

Forced as we are to trust amidst the blast

Our reason and the stars, our fortune cast

On the great deep, the common law of God.

Weak are our doubts. You to your age will prove

Though laws rule here below, they serve above,

That faith will follow upon real insight,

That greater knowledge does but deepen love,

That truths, though different, are ever right,

As all the various colours are but light,

That as each conquest in its turn is new

Cosmos.

It wants for nourishment thought fresh and true
Around the roots from which it rose and grew.

Forgive me, Poet, if I dull thy strain
By artless musings from an o'er-worked brain ;
If I, but tempered by an earthly fire
And gifted only with a babbling tongue,
Should vex thy muse, profane the heavenly lyre,
Haunting its spheres of sound with prattle vain,
Should try with weakling wings the gods among
To rise upon the theme you would inspire,
Forgive me for the love I do not feign ;
When music thrills a human heart for long,
The listener's lips hold echoes of the song,
Murmur its burden though his hearers tire.
Lead thou, O Love, my voice within thy choir,

*   *   *   *

*   *   *   *

*   *   *   *

Placed on the outside of our globe we get

Cosmos. 11

But shore-tossed lava from its tidal core,

Laid in star-spaces and light-film, we let

Our sight search worlds to which we cannot soar,

Between the heavens and earth on watch we're set

All things to challenge, reason of, explore,

So should not, pondering all we see, regret,

If life gives vision, it gives little more.

All the old riddles that bewray our race,

Its conquests far abroad, its wrecks import,

Shew that our strength and weakness interlace,

Shew that our eyes reach far, our arms full short.

Of what I've seen some little would I trace.

    I give a voice then to the wind-drummed sea,

Paint the sun's flush of light from pole to pole,

And sound the spirit for its mystery ;

I draw, I model outlines of the whole,

Life in relief, thought telling of a soul ;

Wandering our island, seaboard's stopping place,

Cosmos.

Its bounds I note, its outlooks into space,

And map the survey in my little scroll,

Writing the marvels as they wrought on me,

Reading the whole of life's grand symphony,

My pipe over the score tripping apace.

Thus in these lines the world itself must sigh,

Its people, not mere heroes, live and die,

Dwarfed, grouped as in their landscape they would lie ;

Clouds must arise, must mass, meet, glow, disperse,

Be heard the silence of the starry sky,

Be felt the wonder of the universe,

As I the oft-told tale in song rehearse

Of man and nature in times far and nigh,

As spring by spring the cuckoo brings his cry.

My arguments I take from all who give,

My instances from out the Seërs' sieve,

I do but set them all to let them live.

But who are Seers, what their prophecy ?

Cosmos. 13

Firing the world by day there strikes the eye

The chariot of the sun ablaze, by night,

Piercing the veil of blue, shy peeps of sight,

As if a naked presence would pass by,

Until the huntress queen of chastity,

Breasting through heaven's phosphorescent sea,

Floods o'er the earth opaque her lucent light.

So far each simple soul can testify.

But look with Seërs' eyes upon the vault,

Its arch withdraws to interstellar space,

And all its sparkling grains of crystal salt

Are lines of light-waves flowing on your face,

Light-waves that ever cross earth's little isle

Quick as a lady's eye her lover's glance,

From far-off suns that gave their present smile

When man himself was not as yet, perchance ;

Look with his eyes upon the ground, you find

Old architectures grow from stage to stage,

Cosmos.

Their orders found, their sculptures so combined

As still to bear the touch of their own age,

And tell the story none could have divined;

Remains of yore bedded in rock and slime,

Fragrant yet with the life-breath of their prime,

Quenched lamps, whose light he brings from buried
time ;

Look with his eyes on reptile, bird, fish, beast,

They are no longer common or unclean,

A miracle is working in the least,

In all the movement of a law is seen ;

You watch their changes and intelligence,

Instinct inherited when life began;

You trace their nearing human shape and sense,

And leap the narrow gulph from them to man ;

And then, as if your prison bars he'd ope,

He will resolve to elements the earth,

Shew sky between each atom's envelope,

Cosmos. 15

And fix each body's mutual weight and worth

Within the chemical kaleidoscope.

His instances out-light a poet's trope.

    Such are the conquests of our prophet-band,

Made whilst we live in thought as each thinks well,

Midst Philistines who only buy and sell

Work, goods or brains, rank, daughters, or their
       land,

Toiling how best their rivals to repel,

Made by our judges, men without command,

Whose word is potent because never planned,

Fresh-fetched from regions where they really dwell,

Who to the host their hard-won secrets tell,

As settlers, where the virgin forests stand,

Let in the light around the trees they fell ;

Seërs who see but not the unseen strand ;

For as the queen of night turns to the sun

In full-orbed radiance whereër he goes,

Cosmos.

Though scarce her profile oft to us she shews,
Though guides may be at fault and we undone,
So other light than nature's Seërs shun,
The cold, reflected sunlight the moon throws
From the lone height of day that she has won,
The kindling picket-light of mountain snows
Revealing to the vales each dawn begun;
And yet how fresh the vision they disclose,
How splendidly their world evolves and grows.

*   *   *   *

*   *   *   *

The sight first in our time that Seërs see
By aid of every side-light, every ray,
Is the earth, a planet, from the sun set free,
Placed, poised, attended as it is to-day,
A fragment of the fire that served the prime,
Still ringing to the stars responsive chime,
Its substance fused, alive, a molten sea,

Cosmos. 17

A plastic lump, as if of potter's clay,

Spinning, revolving at stupendous pace,

Asleep with silent, swift rapidity,

Drawing the cycles whence we draw our time,

A point's point in immensity of space,

A barren world upon a barren chase,

Yet swathed with light and shade of future clime ;

Sheer matter, as a head without a face,

Lifeless as marble, simple, strange, sublime.

How long the fires within, without our sphere,

Were fashioning, before its chain-mailed robe

Was forged amidst the cooling of the globe,

Is known not even to the wisest Seër,

Who sees some hundred million years ago

Its metalled vapours into air get clear,

Its heaviest substance to its centre thrust,

Its fluid mass take film, scum seethe to crust

That quaking bursts, falls to the ebb below,

Cosmos.

Its table-lands arise o'er ocean's flow

And to the shrinking core themselves adjust,

Its squeezed-out mountains bearing on their brow

Their former sweat transformed into snow

By colds of space that weather out their bust,

Its fog-chilled waters and dried foam of dust,

Its draining streams wearing the flooded lea,

Its lands raised from and settling to the sea,

And all in circulation ceaselessly,

Its frost drive in the plough, root out the heat,

Grip half the world and grind as small as sleet :

And then at last, but neither when nor how,

But over all and by the waters rife

And crowning all, the flower-seed we call life,

A rainbow issue of the water-wife,

Got by the heavens above out of the earth below,

From germs the sunbeams brought, the ground made
 grow,

Cosmos. 19

Tinct with their worlds beyond the coloured bow;
That, woven in yet out of matter's mesh,
Which gathered of its store to store afresh,
Clothing the faceless head with living flesh;
Life with its double sex, food, growth, and pride,
Its parts, its splendours, and its times of tide,
Its death with myriad seedlings by its side;
Life so serene that only the rains weep,
Only the winds the seeds of harvest reap,
Only the unwrecked ocean-waves beseech,
Passed amidst silence such as streams still keep,
The vocal silence of the unseen beach,
Swelling round beauty unprofaned by speech,
Round hills of trees whose every leaf's asleep,
Whose plaid of shadow dreams along the reach.

Earth's oped dark lantern's distant, fitful light
Then shews another gift, a greater change,
Creatures with locomotion, appetite,

Cosmos.

As flowers had wished and fluttered into flight,
Over the world its still life re-arrange,
In water, land, and air by spawn, swarm, brood,
Instinct with power to hunt their several food,
With will to struggle for their livelihood,
With sleep, the truce when life and death unite,
Guarded, goaded by pain, by pleasure wooed;
Life with all kinds of form, each with its own,
In strict entail—some now, though changed, are known,
Some from our ocean-flows unchanged are drawn.
From out the head of flesh was found a face
Sightless though seeing, clad with satyr grace
And all the senses of a simple race.
The Seër counts the growths through which he climbs,
But tries in vain to learn the many times
The star-like dawn felt Phosphor pass on high,
The sunsets blushed, the new moons lit the sky—
The moon now shrouded as Pompeii,

Cosmos.

Then full of life perchance as Italy—

Whilst creature-life, as if in pantomimes,

Disported on the scene with wanton cry ;

How often on clear nights the meteors,

Steered by its planets from the nearest sun,

Fresh from their journey of a million years,

Flashed o'er the earth the speed they backwards
　　　spun ;

How oft the circling seasons tilled the land,

Seas shed their oozy skins and shifted place,

Epochs of fire or frost changed nature's face

As the sun changed his colour in mid space,

And ocean's currents commerced on the strand,

Whilst the Creator here but shewed His hand,

With beasts of prey for earth's most favoured race,

Its loveliness their kennel and their chase,

Whilst fancy in the beast awoke desire,

And beauty shone, but none beheld her grace,

Cosmos.

Flowers insects ravished but unseen expire,

Whilst but from cloud or mountain-cone came fire.

  As if the Light unseen of all had sunned

The earth so long that it must burst to flame,

Or spirits that had our dull planet shunned

Were sent to touch the eyes with sight, there came

Thus late upon the stage so long adjusted,

And furnished with his breath, his arms, his pelf,

Man, the learner man, with sense entrusted

To measure all things and to see himself—

Man with his social mate, his queen, his elf;

There bloomed the flower prepared from nature's

      prime,

In thought that glowed with consciousness and awe,

In will that worked to seed each fruit or flaw

There shone in body, bare, erect, and slim,

A brain that mirrored all within its brim,

With range beyond the mere use of a limb—

Cosmos.

The lion milked the cow and cleaned the land,

And rose and led the lightnings by the hand !

The head at large, set free from space and time,

Passed at its will through every age and clime,

Saw with their eyes the things its fellow saw,

Chose, pressed to abstract all it cared to draw,

And worked its way from instances to law,

Living, when dead, in symbol and in rhyme ;

The head at home, subject to time and space,

Took the sharp lines of limit they would trace,

Let their still humour pass into its face.

But then though man was to his life in bond,

His years mature armed him with reach beyond,

With soul of love that fired his clay-wrought wings

To rise above the wisest use of things,

To beat beyond his wants, beyond his sight,

To feel the sweep of greater good than right,

To pass in all things to the infinite ;

24 *Cosmos.*

Or with lust's soul that drove his winged clay
To flutter o'er the ground his wants to feed,
So that heaven's winds unsteady him, impede,
Having no other goal than his own way,
Degrading every appetite to greed.
Man with his inner life, his flesh and bone,
That, as an artist's medium and art,
Parts though they are yet never are apart,
Both joining in the touch of every tone—
The heir-loomed organ with its range of voice
The gift to all, but the lithe, subtle choice
And soul melodious, each master's own ;
And various were the modes in which he played
Before his shadow vanished into shade—
The solo by ambition's trumpet blown,
Affection's fugue deepened by passion's stop,
Crime's startling discord, airs that charmed the fop,
The bass, weird dirge mad superstition made ;

Cosmos. 25

And as each master spoke earth gave her aid
And, listening, joined in concert as he led.
But man, victor of all within his sight,
Had in his heart an unseen world to fight,
Had starry heavens unknown of pagan light.

Then was there born the glory of all time,
Then shone supreme Creative Love sublime,
Then reached us, bearing heaven in his span,
Our living Word divine, the perfect man,
And God was known and holiness began.

Such stages in the world's past course we spy,
We search out how they came, we reason why,
Nay ponder whence, whene'er at fate we pluck—
Fate, phantom shade cast round us from on high
Horizon-like, that cannot be passed by,
In whose elastic cloud-cloak we are stuck ;
Yet as our brain sees farther than our eye,
Although we fail to find, we ever try.

Cosmos.

Why law, mind without muscle, ruled, not luck,

Earth answered sky with spontaneity,

The sun and moon o'er-ruled each drop of sea,

And each thing to its neighbour tried to get,

How they had separate notes, and as two met

Why they both changed so that a chord was struck,

None know, we see that thus things ever do.

How matter's chords were then with music sped,

The music being other yet inbred,

With leaves that lived and flowers that seemed to love,

Or why these plants upon moist mould had fed

With roots below and bloom and fruit above,

None know; we say that vegetables grow.

And from this music how there rose a song,

Apart, pathetic, native, that ne'er ceased,

The voice of throbbing bird or bellowing beast,

How each with sense innate was borne along

To his own place at nature's tontine feast,

Cosmos. 27

Not one of all their offspring coming wrong,

None know ; we say that animals breed so.

Then how there came the leader of the choir,

Man, the conductor, with harmonious soul

Reading the score, feeding each part with fire,

Yet rising with the music o'er the whole,

Know none, not though an ape's ape had a son,

No more than how the course could have begun.

And, lastly, how the perfect one became,

Know none; we see the world charged with his name,

Feel at its sight intolerable shame.

  *   *   *   *

Life makes us work, and as we work we know :

We reap our father's, our fore-father's corn

And plant for our descendants yet unborn

The knowledge they will thrash out and re-sow ;

We have to make our malt and fill our horn,

Though facts may fail we cannot thought forego.

Cosmos.

Thus in our daily task-work we are led
From all our fresh-found facts aside to turn,
To watch the bush on fire that does not burn,
The power that is not chance in all inbred—
What is? that halts not, sleeps not, nor is fed,
That holds unseen our ashes in their urn,
That was in all before the seas were spread,
And would be if all living things were dead?
What it to us and we to it, we'd learn:
Thus seeking everywhere the will divine
That shows itself abroad in awful sign,
Far as the farthest-sighted star-lamps shine.

Supreme o'er all we find a ruling care,
A providence whose order all things share,
That to the stars adjusts their age, food, train,
How sun, earth, moon, shall on each other bear,
That sends the springs and rivers to the main,
Its briny waters to the cloudy plane,

Cosmos.

The sweetened clouds to fall in fertile rain,

The freshness of the morning to the air,

The earth the seed it multiplies to grain,

Its pose that brings our seasons to the year,

The eye the sight to read the distant glare,

The meaning of the sense-nerves to the brain,

Each life its instincts, structure, the whole chain,

The correlations that can keep it fair,

The energy that need do naught again,

That stores whatever waste is caused by wear,

Suffering loss, to turn it into gain,

With patience everlasting arms sustain,

That through the storm or calm but seems to
change,

Constant with sunshine as with shadows strange,

That never fails throughout its endless range ;

A care with rules so sure we name them laws,

So faultlessly enforced we call them cause,

30 *Cosmos.*

So wide that in dead things they store the force
Which in the living burns out in discourse :
One fountain feeding all from its one source.

But then as matter is inspired with life,
Has inward motions that it must disburse,
And units rise upon the universe
With signs of purpose almost over-rife,
A blight appears, a parasite, a curse,
With freedom, freedom also to coerce,
Antagonisms, fear and mortal strife,
Where beaks and claws and teeth forestall the knife,
Nor any test of better or of worse,
With drugs and poisons thick in nature's purse,
Than the raw power of which war is the nurse,
Or than the choice that makes a maid a wife,
Though everywhere prolific creatures teem
Whose days of brightness scarce their night redeem ;
Till in one life all oppositions throng

Cosmos. 31

Focussed within, than life or death more strong,

And man is polarised to right and wrong;

As if within his worlds, to let life grow,

There must be room for choice, be bad and good,

Pressure, fecundity, solicitude,

Be fulness brimming on to overflow,

The life-seeds given as the winds that blow,

As if man's worth is earth's until applied,

His innocence mere ignorance till tried,

His gold but clay sun-pierced and purified.

Thus ere an angel could have blushed for man

Rough competition and sharp pain began,

The sacrifice of life was nature's plan,

And age on age, ere man received his breath,

Brute generations fed the earth with death;

The wave of life sank in the sea beneath.

Nature, more liberal of life than food,

Lets but the fittest linger with their brood,

Cosmos.

Fresh-clothes her form as man renews his mood,

But hides from all all knowledge of their end

Except from him whose aims his life transcend,

Who, too, with tears and laughter can unbend.

Thus matter's force threw foam-like life ashore

On the earth-reef the high tides over-bore,

And instinct set it playing on the beach,

And when the tides had all within their reach

They changed the waifs that they had brought before;

But when as well as instinct there was man,

The foam-life was the boat on matter's sea

Which he could navigate, the reef to scan,

The stars and winds to learn; his course was free,

Fishing the waters as they round him ran,

To sail them for the land where he would be,

The land they rest upon, whence they began,

Where his Creator is, his destiny.

Yet is man subject to the power unknown

Cosmos. 33

That sorts the world with its machinery,

Is forced its old prerogative to own,

Ordained when God of matter made His throne

And gave it properties wherewith to ply ;

He has to learn it cannot hear his cry,

Requires obedience, not agony,

Obedience that nought else can atone,

Nor tender ignorance, nor sweetest moan,

Nor constancy of service life-long grown,

Nor all the arts a cunning head may try :

The power as law that gives to him alone

Who reads the order and the purpose shewn,

When knowledge with obedience will vie,

The rule on earth, the message from the sky ;

The law once fate throned o'er the highest high ;

The laws despotic o'er the world of things,

Incarnate in the vital worlds that die,

That never rest or change, are ever nigh—

34 *Cosmos.*

Power-spirits and blind inward motionings
Whose roots as rays, whose leaves as sunbeams glance,
Each fixed as fate, all flexible as chance,
Fresh-focussed by each moving circumstance,
That leave in man his joys and sufferings,
The discipline of choice his freedom brings,
The conscious life from which his conscience springs ;
Laws he may guide, make, as it were, connive
By setting context with its text to strive,
That ne'er relent nor ever can forgive ;
That make him free because they let him trust,
That let him wiser grow, by them he must,
That may be cruel but are always just.

Yet man of laws to reach within has need,
Laws that can guide him trembling with desire,
When vile oppression makes him intercede,
Or all his life is lit with love's own fire,
Writ by a heart like his but purer, higher ;

Cosmos.

For nature's laws were never yet his creed;
He 's that within by which he must aspire,
Which outstrips nature's laws in every deed
By which a man his fellow men can lead.
When to this inner life he makes appeal,
The life of which his body is the guise,
The life which death itself can neither steal
Nor work up into nature's merchandise,
Though he by means of nature's spells upsprings,
He finds he's their magician not their slave,
A person moving in the realm of things,
Dazzled yet wanting what they never gave,
The touch of soul for which his heart must crave,
Of soul that neither wealth nor beauty brings.

    Thus although nature has her own fixed laws
Which at man's vice or virtue never pause,
The good man in defeat yet hears applause,
The bad one in success heart-prickings strange :

36   *Cosmos.*

Though nature works with elemental strife
Ever evolving, interchanging life,
It builds a higher on a lower range,
And changing is regenerate with change.
First matter came instinct with varied force,
Then plants and animals had intercourse,
At last free-will brought marriage and divorce.
For nature is of man the mermaid wife
And mother of the birth divine, the heir
That men with joy regret, with sorrow bear,
Till love and hope outgrow the burden care,
And they can use the sacrificial knife
Their self-regarding habit-shoots to pare,
To cut off hate which leads but to despair,
Till in their child divine their joys are rife ;
Thus magically should man's brief time wear,
To such high end be wedded nature fair.

The seeming level lengths of nature's plains

Cosmos.

Lead to a Mind, a Will that o'er it reigns :

Amidst its myriad works we find our brains,

Our numbers, forms, our reason's counterpart,

The laws at work whence science draws her chart,

The beauty and variety of art,

Our statesmen's foresight, our schoolmasters' pains,

A wealth, a waste of life at which we start,

A limitless command of time and means,

The present world which we must make our mart,

The stars which hold our losses or our gains—

All but the god-like soul, all but the loving heart.

*   *   *   *

*   *   *   *

*   *   *   *

The heart, the soul, from what source do they flow ?

Of man we try to learn how thought unfurled

When the sun's rescue gave the morning glow,

Its early death in glory was a woe,

Cosmos.

When the first words were struck, the first tales trolled,

When gods in guise of men were friend and foe,

And hero-chiefs their children here below,

And by our Seërs' help we learn to know.

Glimpses we gain of boyish days of yore,

Only our race's childhood's blotted o'er.

We learn to trace the story of our world

Wherein, without our choice, we're born, we grow,

In whose environment we are uncurled,

To which our life's outfit, outlook we owe ;

And as before its time its age grows more,

Its waste lands settled, all its peoples known,

We make the distant countries share their store,

We bring the past years nearer to our own,

And feed upon the fruits of every zone.

Our past, our present life we now explore.

Man found the earth a virgin mine unwrought,

Its surface a mere play-ground for wild game,

Cosmos.

He wandered far and by all things was taught,

And as he learned they ceased to be the same ;

He dressed the land, the fruits came forth he sought,

He fed the beasts, the flocks he sought for came ;

All was his own, for all he could reclaim ;

He multiplied and found his wants augment,

He hunted moor and wood with son and sire,

With bribe and fine his brain was made invent,

His women digging roots tilled as they went,

His gesture, word, his sign told his intent,

Ambition ever led him to acquire,

And from his smouldering heat would leap the fire,

The light divine, the very heavens inspire.

For man groping in fog of ignorance,

E'er sorted what he saw with reason's glance,

Feeling a wrong would make deliverance.

His outward gifts, his various inner sight,

Spread him abroad the lord of all the lands,

40 *Cosmos.*

The barrier waters bore him to their strands;

His story could be told; from head and hands,

Tools and adventurers came and proved his might;

The woods fell down and gave him up their light,

And as his labours spoke earth heard commands

And answered them with treasures infinite

From times when it was wrapped in swathing bands.

Through the primæval forest's night-like shade,

Where beast and reptile had long lurked and preyed,

Day broke at last, and open ways were made.

Such was man's work, his wants his talents taught;

But then besides his will and passions grim,

He 'd hear a voice within tell him he ought,

Be led by what to all but him was nought,

Give up to others that which he had sought.

His parents, wife, and child, were nearest him

And faith in them made fear of kindred dim,

At last relationship included whim.

Cosmos. 41

Life's little wants cooperation caught,

Its great fused the tribe's body, forged the limb,

And gave to each the shield of all the lot,

The common social rights that were begot—

The child, the strength with which the warrior fought,

The man the comradeship by trials bought ;

And life in families toned mind by mind,

Moulded the plastic soul in youth inshrined,

And as the strong ones were the more refined

The love of self to self-respect was brought

And self-respect with sacrifice was fraught,

And men became the workmen of mankind,

And loving music, colour, form or thought

Gave up to all the fine arts that they wrought.

Thus by the gifts of individual eyes,

By play of sex and race, life's legacies,

Man's common sight was widened, he grew wise.

Man, the most widely social being known,

Cosmos.

Within his several worlds would live alone,

Each doing as he chose, or wrong or right ;

Although his race, sex, country, time and light,

Were fixed on each as harness for the fight,

He fought his battle with his sling and stone,

And made his real, his inner life his own ;

And gave expression to his flesh and bone.

Lived bodiless to Him, the One unseen,

Who found him life and all its store of food,

Had of his own what he had done, had been,

His choice, his love of what to him was good—

The quarter seasons chiming his short day

From weakness into strength, on to decay,

As gently as the shadows round a bay,

The boisterous spring singing its jolly call,

Summer's full moon of work and warmth and flowers,

The harvest-home and halo of the fall,

And winter's stooping sun and snow-lit hours,

Cosmos. 43

Ringing their changes to his changing powers.

Was the first life on earth the same as ours?

The same in substance, simpler in its form;

Our changes grow, for there is no return,

No living in nor yet without the past,

And every age has its own self to learn,

And truth the life beyond the age to last.

Comparing men from farthest, yet-known time,

They differ less than in a fresh-made place,

Where our own age o'erlaps the boyish prime,

Less than from homes or haunts of worth or crime,

The members manifold but one the race,

With brain-power savages cannot efface,

Franchised with speech, signed by the human face.

The trappers who made stones do their behest,

The cunning craftsmen who a metal dressed,

The men who led the world on Egypt's mires,

The Indians, descendants of the sires

Cosmos.

Of all our sovran nations of the west,

The myriads of the oldest of empires,

The Jewish prophet and the Grecian sage,

The men who kept our world so long in thrall—

We see them as the children of their age,

We feel we are the kindred of them all,

Flush when they're great, nay, blush when they are
      small;

We who, wild, civilized, or slave or free,

Or in our nature's scope or mystery

Scarce change with time more than the land or sea.

One only o'er his age, sex, country stood,

And to man's soul revealed the heart of God.

   Meanwhile man's fate was as his conduct had,

Though fortune's hand was oft forced by the bad—

The years with rooted force the races clad.

Conquered by force or luck and ruled by fear,

  Men settled into layered castes severe,

Cosmos.

Which mellowed into forms and manners sere;

Then customs grew to laws to be obeyed,

Ideals into fetishes were made,

Man's stock would be both growing and decayed.

And he of every creature differed most

In sweep of height to rise, of depth to fall,

And less in fortune's gifts than natural;

War to the peoples was a holocaust,

It welded, trained them, though it would exhaust,

The man of parts would have the foremost post;

Captives for slavery not slaughter call,

Rude slavery which masters might enthrall;

Although the lord might take, the slave lose all,

Yet as man's years were few all was not lost;

Evil flushed with its own success would brawl,

Though wickedness would promise it would pall;

Time proved that work, peace, wit were worth their

cost,

46 *Cosmos.*

Time would e'en prove each nation's life and worth,

That failing when this died of utter dearth,

On land laid stark by man's mad fire or frost,

A plague in mercy burying the host,

A better people coming to the birth.

Although of war and chase men made their boast,

Yet as they spread the richer grew the earth.

   *   *   *   *

Man is humane though history records.

Waste seems to us, as colour to the blind,

The times on earth when thought was not, nor
   words,

Nor any singing but the pipe of birds,

Nor listeners but the mocking hills or herds,

Nor music but of water or of wind—

Music the spirit-fire lit by mankind :

Empty earth's stage would seem if man were not,

Though perfect beauty glowed upon the scene,

Cosmos.

Though nymphs or fawns or fairies filled his lot

In want of nothing, and without or blot,

Or mirage-haunting memories of a spot;

What food indeed could our heart-hunger glean—

Our life o'er-run by wealth that leaves it lean,

If fruits of spirit-harvests were not seen

Blooming and seeding in our neighbour's plot,

A Mahomet, a Buddha had not been,

Were Socrates, Confucius forgot,

Had He, the holy one, not joined our strife

And shewn the worth of every human life—

A seed from the great Sower's hand out-shot?

To man mind, beauty spiritless is mean,

Though life-like as the last steam-worked machine.

What is the spirit-life, and how begot?

Fires, earthquakes, whirlwinds pass and disappear;

'Tis not from nature's forces nor from fear,

It is from men His still small voice we hear

Cosmos.

Who, Master Spirit, to us all entrusts

That wondrous inner life in which each lives

And through our thoughts such new growth ever
   gives,

Like sunlight in a plant that it adjusts,

So long as one true deed of prayer survives,

As moulds us 'midst life's habits, cares, and lusts,

Amidst the effervescence of a will,

Moved by all motives that the heart can fill,

In opposition none can reconcile—

A growth that lands us where we willed to lie,

But that detains us when we would go thence ;

That yields perchance e'en to Omniscience,

Who sets the needle conscience we steer by

And sees our voyages within His sky,

The freshness of an earthly parent's eye,

The curiosity of our suspense—

An inner life, focus of mind and sense,

Cosmos. 49

Fount of our individuality:

A spirit life whose birth is never seen,

Though we see when it is, when it is not,

Whose seat none knows nor how it was begot,

Which comes as man first came upon the scene ;

An inner life so far our life alone

That that is nought to us which is not known,

That only true to us we can believe,

That only even faith we can receive,

That force can fright not, fear cannot improve,

But only love howe'er debased can move ;

A life o'er which such power we each possess

Our every thought leaves in it its impress,

A life such power possessing over each

Which tells our very reason what to teach ;

The life which dwells in nature's flesh and bone

And fashions them until they are its own,

That chooses at the first and works its thought,

50 *Cosmos.*

And at the last unconsciously is wrought,
That feeds on all, builds all within its frame,
Is ever changing, yet is still the same,
That lives e'en when its body is outworn,
In traits and tastes in issue yet unborn :
For as each life through its worn channel goes,
Tinged with the many soils through which it flows,
Its freighted volume comes from travelled deeps
That memory's association keeps,
And as it seeks fresh ground and gathering grows,
Fertile with blessings or with poisoning woes,
It feeds still from the fount whence it arose,
Still feels the rock, the mount from which it sweeps,
The heaven-fled snows from which its glacier creeps.

Life's course meanders guided by debate ;
For men are made to wrestle for their fate,
They have with persons and with things to strive,
For food to labour, or they cannot live,

Cosmos. 51

For children, to choose out and win a mate,

Provide, maintain, advance and educate ;

Each seeks his own, finds others, joins the state.

Each seeks his welfare and as trade winds blow

Earth-currented and by their constant drift

With streams and eddies " vein the ocean's flow "

And mix the tropic seas and polar snow,

So men in search of gain use every shift

Those steady winds, self-interests, bestow,

Go their own way, the way none else can go,

Seek fortune from afar or save by thrift,

Give all their wants so that they want the gift

And in return give more than they can owe—

Winds of the earth that life's freight waft and sift,

Midst storms of passion that the waters lift—

Winds from above that bear on all below.

Each has his life, yet owns it but by trial ;

The great man's son has starved upon his pile,

Cosmos.

The hero on the poorest soil has thriven,
The hardest lot has room for self-denial,
The scantiest has all its blessings given—
Those that the proudest share with the most vile,
The beauty of the earth and of the heaven.
Man's life-flow may be tainted at its source,
Or circumstance may lead him into ill,
Life starts without or memory or remorse,
Propensities must try, they need not kill,
And if he sees and loves the better course,
Repentance shows he has his own free will,
Living two lives the new one to fulfil,
And martyrdom he need not even bow to force :
The body's tendencies, brain-structure even,
Are by the will to its ideals driven,
Habits by other habits may be riven.
Man, made a husbandman by daily need,
Plants but his fallows as he airs his whim,

Cosmos. 53

And either sows afresh his harvest seed

Or feeds the parasites that feed on him;

From his forced use of will his ways extend

Up life's lit hill down to the valleys dim,

The roads that part determining the end

Where both his life and life-lamp conscience wend—

Conscience, whose virgin lamp kept trimmed aright,

Sheds over man the rays of God's own light,

Awakens him to see that love is sight.

And in man's moral life there is no waste,

His good and bad are kept and interlaced,

He is himself the life he has embraced.

Thus he keeps building up his choice afresh

Until his inner life is clothed in flesh,

That inner life in which we each can see

The justest liberty that here may be,

The clear approach e'en to equality—

For in its magic mirror all is seen,

54 *Cosmos.*

Hid skeletons of heart and brain appear,
Deep wells of love and hate that never were,
Past embryoes of births that have not been,
And songs unsung, and griefs without a tear,
And over all the heaven of each man's prayer.
But then man's life and inner life between
May not fell circumstances intervene?
More is he than the sum of what has been?

No outward pressure drives man to transgress;
Life's ills may maim him, yet he does not fall
Till he enslaves himself, is his own thrall,
Till only evil gives him taste at all.
Grim poverty may grip him in its press,
Care well nigh choke him, all things seem to pall,
And yet when most benumbed by littleness,
And mesmerised by sameness near and small,
Affliction, sorrow, rousing him may bless
With patience in, then pity for, distress—

Cosmos. 55

Sorrow that comes up like a flood at night,

And lays around him its unearthly light,

Or baseness may awake him when he's swooned,

Sin startling him to life with poisoning wound,

If to a higher tone his heart's attuned,

If, when he's facing wrong that's done on high,

He scorns the meanness, and he hates the lie.

When his beloved are strangled by disease

In saint-borne sufferings nothing can appease,

It is not wrath that rises from lost love,

He'd sooner death than vice his children seize ;

Lust murders, and escapes with cunning ease,

Not rage and terror only his heart move

As if the end were here and not above,

Here justice is blindfolded, there she sees.

Each of us in our little universe,

In any region where our heart is struck,

Though the sun shines upon the common ruck,

56 _Cosmos._

Finds better than mere better, worse than worse,

Foreshadowed finds or promise or a curse

Bred from the soul, that is not fate nor luck,

Whose final fruit this life can never pluck.

The mountain strength may labour with a mouse,

And virtue have at least its share of woe,

But though the world should seem one big hot-house

And providence the force that makes things grow,

We have the Sower's foresight of the show

And cry for justice e'en in fame below,

Carrying all our life on to its close

For restitution, progress, soul-repose.

Our world is not the best one we would know.

Here peaceful patriots for their country fall

And women suffer most when soldiers fire,

Rare genius as 'tis speaking may expire,

And the poor neighbour who has lent his all

Can when in want nor borrow nor recall,

Cosmos.

57

And bad men through long life have their desire,

Whilst good ones smile in marble at their sire,

And oft our dearest by deceit appal;

And thus our spirit looks beyond our life,

Makes but its earthy root by earthly strife,

Breathes through its leaves—the good to others done,

But stays its bloom for its life-promised sun;

Though even here worth has a present gain,

So much so that men test, nor all in vain,

Right by its colour joy, wrong by its shadow pain.

Although the earth as if prepared for man

Had been with metals, coal, grain, cattle stored,

And men who ever multiplied the hoard

And throve as with the course of things they ran,

Had gathered of the grapes, had feasted Pan,

We laud the goodness of another Lord,

Find more than food in nature's wide domain,

More in the stars and clouds than light and rain,

Cosmos.

In music, colour, more than sound and stain,

Feel interest in all the brutes and flowers—

Within our power they are beyond our powers,

The works of One whose work is not as ours,

Whose presence is and yet does not appear,

Whom men at best in some mode must revere.

For we, the highest of all creatures here,

And amongst us the man of finer make,

Alone of all the creatures in our sphere

Have a life-thirst we must, we cannot slake,

A lack, a longing want, dull, deep, austere—

Of which power, pleasure, wealth but hide the ache,

And health and earthly love themselves partake,

That only duty moves and makes more clear,

Have a free spirit high enough to break,

Yet have to wait and toil o'er each day's stake,

To waste and wear our life, to wind and veer,

To win what good we can, make that most dear,

Cosmos.

Our first fond fancy lose, our home forsake,

For though our life's a dream we are awake

And hear when all too late what wisdom spake.

Yet should our heart, come worse, come worst, faint

    ne'er,

God's day-spring shines us hope beyond our fear,

Hope, rainbow-like, that would transmute our tear :

When the worse Cæsar his great triumphs had,

Our statesman, to his country only wed,

Heart-broken though the war was to be won,

Despairing died by his despair misled ;

A widow, dying, to the stranger said,

Still tending on her one, long-buried son,

" You'll promise, now I've told you of the lad,

" To think of him sometimes when I am gone ?"

Is hope in life, is hope in death undone ?

What are the grounds of hope we rest upon ?

What is our knowledge worth ?   Whence is it drawn ?

Cosmos.

Knowledge of letters and of sciences—

Letters the leavings of our human tide,

rience—the progress of appearances—

Feeds man, but leaves him still unsatisfied,

What he knows, what he knows not, inhances ;

He tries all ways and means to pass inside

To where all truths in harmony abide,

The central source whence thought and things out-

        glide.

The tidings science brings are true, if slight,

Although her footing's mortal in its might,

Tho' faith is wanted to attest her sight.

Even the raised views of nature's reign

That shape themselves within the minds of men,

Though bounded by the circle of their ken

And tinted with the tone of each one's brain,

Are true as men themselves are true and sane.

To them the earth stands still although it moves,

Cosmos. 61

The sun moves round them though 'tis standing still,

The stars are fixed round which all planets file,

Though sun, stars, planets fly through space in
    droves ;

Truth's aspects shift as facets of a hill.

True are the living types that letters leave,

The insight to the life of which they weave,

The spirit by whose light all men perceive.

Thus from man's many-posted points of sight

There slowly breaks with more than local light

Fresh, final knowledge from the infinite ;

Thus o'er his name, his work will sometimes be,

Despite the little while men may agree,

A human tinge of immortality.

If told his knowledge is of lengths of light,

Of shorter lengths of sound in waves of flight,

Of touch, taste, smell, reports of matter's plight—

Sensations these, succeeding touches those,

62 *Cosmos.*

He says if these are all men's minds inclose

The fauna, the flora know as he knows :

Things pass, his nerves but tell him they have been,

It is by thought relationships are seen,

Thought that links 'fore and aft with cause between.

If told he thinks but knows not, should not try

But eat and help his brother till all die,

And make mankind at large his only shrine,

Ignoring the unknown, the night's design,

He sees the heavens, believes they do not lie,

The heavens unveiled at eve to touch his eye,

And asks " O man, amidst the stars that shine,

Dost think there is no wit, no heart but thine?"—

There is that is, and men are not, divine ;

For nature's works his own conceits disperse,

And he, at highest, freed from every curse,

Is but a babe lost in the universe.

Through space, through time, if haply he may find,

Cosmos. 63

He seeks the spirit-world, unseen, behind,

The world that makes, preserves, and takes his kind.

Though from his seeking sight may stand apart,

The kingdom of his God is in his heart,

And listening for the everlasting Word

Amidst the schooling of his petty cries,

He hears the wisdom that the ages heard

And sees the worlds to come within the skies,

Learns from what is, and, working it, grows wise.

Man's future, brought him by the world above

Whence came his reason and the things of sense,

Lies in that consciousness of sovran love

His helplessness from in the womb inwove,

Which trusts its object, not its evidence—

That world above whose outward shows and light

His mind deciphers, his eyes read aright,

Whose fruits and seasons in their own time traced

The forest sky in which Earth's nest is placed.

64 *Cosmos.*

Thus wistful, conscious of his littleness,

Strong in God's strength, of all truths he takes hold,

Too weak to know, too strong to merely guess,

He searches out the people's heart of old,

True, stubborn, sinning, willing to confess,

Whose granite wills heaven's sweetest flowers enfold,

Supreme, as Greeks in art, in godliness,

Who seeking found the Unseen in their distress,

Whose poets, prophets, his best life express;

And, drinking in the lightning of their stroke,

He finds his spirit tenanted by sight,

And though the depths but by faint stars are broke,

Though he's climbed through the clouds and it is night,

Though utter distance weights him with its cloak

And tempts to sleep from which none are awoke,

He's nerved to follow what he knows is right,

To go where he can see, to bear the yoke

That conscience pointed to when conscience spoke,

Cosmos. 65

And so his patient longing for more light

Grows ever surer and more infinite.

The Lord of all, his soul's Lord he must own,

He is no longer in the world alone.

He sees amidst life's sodden misery,

Amidst the wealth of thrift's too sordid greed,

For better and for worse as men are free,

For richer, poorer, they are one Sire's seed,

Must live as brothers if as sons they plead.

And then he finds the treasure he had sought,

The man of men in travail of his Lord—

Most lonely, lofty, loving, loved, abhorred—

The very well of water for his drought,

God as a Father to man's heart restored—

So lives in the one life that is for all

Ideal loveliness time cannot pall,

The height to shew the measure of man's fall ;

For as heaven's quiver holds the starry ray,

66 *Cosmos.*

The past preserves Christ's presence, holds his sway,

His light and love, far-reaching, on men play.

   Thus we hear whispers round the heaven's dome

That echo in our hearts with thoughts of home,

True and in search of truth not far we roam—

Truth by whose steadfastness the heavens last,

Immortal as the sky, as oft o'ercast,

And fathomless beyond its treasures vast.

'Tis but by truth of soul that he is known ;

For all who e'er will live of good or rare,

Though him they know not, though they stand alone,

In joy of joy and carelessness of care,

In ever helping others bear, forbear,

Draw in his spirit's life-renewing air,

Breathe out the foulness that is all their own ;

We men are trusted with the seed he's sown,

Trusted to dress the soil in which 'tis grown,

And thus our fate is in our own decree,

Cosmos. 67

To desecrate our spirit's liberty
Or make whatever would be best to be.

Thus is the higher life denied to none,
Is by the simplest life-long service won;
Thus all who keep alive their brothers' lives
Live as he lived, survive as he survives,
When this life ends the little they have done,
And the next brings for every living one
The increase that God giveth unto souls,
The growth in being as by daily doles,
The seeing Him in that which He controls,
As He proceeds with that which He's begun.
Here, now, we even faintly see our goals—
Our earthly flowers are drawn out by the sun,
The sun far-off round which our planet rolls;
And as the sky is on, is in the earth,
Wields it with forces that in roses hide—
Breathless we hear them o'er the mountains glide—

68 Cosmos.

With light and heat and air of chemic worth,
Electric pulses through the sun's own girth,
With times and seasons and the shifts of tide,
And brings from far the cure for all our dearth,
Revealing the whole universe outside,
Itself impalpable, where all abide—
The spirit-world surrounds us from our birth
And opens to our gaze a space, a time
Where other worlds such workings interweave
As make us with our night at hand believe
That love itself dwells in the void sublime,
Will feed our souls on many an unseen coast
Where the far heavens a higher life inspire ;
That as our sun, seen as night's wandering ghost,
Seems to die daily on its cloudy pyre
Giving its place to all the starry host,
Its sunlight lapsing as in dying ire,
Yet lives below and joins the heavenly choir

Cosmos. 69

With almost all its wondrous wealth of fire,

All but the particles its planets crossed,

Our inner lives—which oft in life seemed lost,

Which life is scarce lit by, can ne'er exhaust,

Which ever radiate and seek their sire

Here in earth-womb with instinct-like desire,

Pass on to Heaven, become what they aspire—

Sunlight that floods the black, blue sky at night

Unseen like love save where it can alight,

The substance all our shadows bring to sight.

*   *   *
*   *   *
*   *   *

Thus, Poet, sounds the music of the spheres

Through all the distance trembling in our ears ;

Our bygone conquests you will not despise

Nor think our broad though broken views unwise,

Because more time will carry with its years

Cosmos.

Some newer problems, interests and fears,
And larger vision and fresh harmonies.
Our warrior Seers now are tracing back
The trail of our existence on the earth,
So as to gain the secret of our birth;
As yet its parentage, its time they lack;
To you the trail may be a well-worn track,
The mode of all our origins be shewn—
Or that all families of life retreat
In separate, level lines that only meet,
Like cloudy sunbeams at their pointed cone,
At the one source from which each starts complete,
Or in the distance from some germ have grown,
Through myriad evolutions yet unknown,
To man through monkey, fish, sponge, grass, or wheat,
Through what at last is nebulæ alone.
A greater Newton may have told for you
The orbit and the weight of every star

Cosmos. 71

Within our galaxy's vast retinue,

Each stellar system in its figure true ;

Drawn constellations as they really are—

To us heaven's avenues, perpetual dew ;

Or shewn what takes a star like Sirius

Big as a thousand times our mighty Sun,

To gravitation self-impervious,

And keeps it shooting space as lightnings run.

Our brains you may have read ; we have divined

That matter moves whenever moves the mind,

E'en when 'tis most at rest, and dreams are spun,

Soul by its body is drawn out and signed.

Born farther in time's course, whilst you will gain

Fresh power from knowledge and a brighter gleam,

And looking back will smile that we complain

Our numbers grow, our coal we can't redeem,

You, though on you beyond or eye or brain

Fresh phases of the niverse will beam,

72   Cosmos.

The side you may not see will seek in vain—
The life to come, the land beyond the main:
In vain you'll try to penetrate in thought
To nature's limit or infinity,
To there where space is not nor time can be,
To whence the world-materials were brought:
What mind, what matter is, how fixed, how taught.

Our Seers say that in the worlds they see
The sum of all cannot be altered aught,
'Tis what it was ere life's first seed was wrought,
That if all life went out 'twould differ not,
That all by conservation is loss free
And must keep so by continuity,
That all through evolution was begot
By correlation's sole paternity
Off time in any length of pedigree—
Time that has changed, lost, multiplied each jot,
Preserved each instinct and matured the lot;

Cosmos. 73

That mind is merely matter at its best,

Or matter only mind made manifest ;

As matter's forces can but interchange,

That all things tend toward a final rest,

An equilibrium of all possessed

With nothing from without to disarrange,

In which each molecule's flittings are compressed,

The Suns moon-cinders cold, dark, death-set, strange,

Bodies with motions gone, beyond decay,

Unburied ghosts that cannot pass away ;

That nature's length of life has but its day ;

That more than nature nature cannot shew ;

There is no more above than is below ;

The supernatural is what none know.

But you, if even you should think this true,

Will seek beyond it for the larger view,

How nature came to bring forth life that grew.

Earth's great mutations ever more complex,

Cosmos.

The building up of mammal life to man,
His education by his world, race, sex,
Shew us the progress that bespeaks a plan—
For matter, material, moves but by laws,
Is but a means, is neither end nor cause.
Suppose our water fails, our oceans sink,
Leaving fast-shrinking mist within the deep-sea's hold,
With arid deserts stretching to the brink,
The mountain-tops with only light to drink,
And earth a larger moon of sandy gold ;
Or say the sun's volcanoes burst their base
And it and all its planets fly to space ;
Yet even if old Chaos were to come,
What power of Cosmos so long banished it ?
What set the mystic dance, the music dumb,
And all the lightning play of human wit ?
Were laws unaimed that nature's nature hit,
Unconsciously that conscience-laws emit?

Cosmos. 75

Does not our life look farther than its day,

Our love last longer than its month of May?

Are life and love but toys to throw away?

E'en if a vapour was condensed to earth,

The stones of earth were ground, and from their paste

All living things were raised, e'en children's mirth.

Man reigns.   E'en if the vapour were replaced,

One must have been on Whom the whole was based,

Who laid and lit the suns that light our hearth,

To Whom space gave no limit, time no haste,

By all law-served, by man alone love-traced,

Most gracious above all that He had graced,

Known as the unknown Fount of all known worth,

The Spirit from whose source all souls flowed forth

And rose in clouds light-pierced but uneffaced,

Rose upwards to the level of their birth.

The dream that dead and live things everywhere

Are but the clustered atoms of the air,

76 *Cosmos.*

Chance-blown, no longer mocks our mind's despair;

By night-mare that necessity has wrought

For every man his every act, word, thought,

These unknown rhymes, yours will not be distraught

Our life is not the flesh from which it springs,

Nor love once lit the sport of beauty's wings;

Though life and love mature, they precede things.

As nature's babes, we gaze at what it saith,

And draw its food till we are weaned by death.

Ah! that by gazing you or I could see,

From nature's whispered hush, what we shall be

When we receive our immortality;

In the great Spring when we have back our breath

And life begins in perpetuity,

When as old earth of yore by fire once fused,

The ages bring us gifts that will be used

When with the starry cycles we shall share

The final issue to which all things bear,

Cosmos. 77

And nothing will be wasted or abused,

When we shall see the light in blackness sheer,

Each altar-star ablaze, all beauties bare,

Suns of all colours, not hope's rainbowed air—

The halo-promise of our atmosphere.

Now God withdraws Himself to let us grow

Wise in our will by reaping what we sow,

Then, if we may not see Him, we shall know

It was in love He let us build our fate,

Our outer to our inner life translate,

Designed that we should fashion, He create.

Now we see everything with our own eyes,

And then how can we see ought otherwise?

Oh! how shall we, whose eyes are crime, lust, pelf?

What can we outside-seeing mortals say

Of him who sacrifices to himself,

That weakest idol of untempered clay,

When selfishness itself has passed away?

78 *Cosmos.*

Of him who rising from earth's covering sod
Would sooner see his devil than see God ?
O sense-bound as we are, our earthly life
Sand,—roped by continuity of strife,
A flame that must be fed incessantly,
How can we see ourselves set free from sense,
Gazing at truth and not at evidence ?
How can we see ourselves from time set free,
Being, not having been, and but to be ?—
One life speaks to us o'er the grave's dead sea.

When man and nature's source is seen as one,
And that one source is seen to be divine,
We can take home the life divinely run,
Its sky, its ocean breadth, its mountain line,
Can see by its own light it is God's son,
The light those see who cannot see it shine.
The light may seem far off, inadequate,
Yet life within each soul it can create ;

Cosmos. 79

What though the life was mortal in its day ?

It lives, its life we cannot solve, gainsay.

The soul both so supremely sweet and great,

We take its witness whatsoe'er it state ;

The soul of one who felt no stain of clay,

Of one who stood o'er all, yet joined the fray,

One, the one man, to whom a man can pray.

We long for, may you live the life he crowned,

Make come the kingdom that he came to found,

See love and peace, not greed and war, abound.

Nor because love is good should we have fear ;

Our sight though weak is true within its range ;

The Light of all the suns, when we come near,

The Light unseen that maketh all appear,

Will leave our point of sight amidst all change ;

The planet's glow is of the sun's own sphere.

As Seërs find earth's metals in a star,

We feel the love in which the angels are ;

Cosmos.

Mere seedlings of the earth, our hearts, our eyes,
Live in the Light that ever shines on them,
Bloom in the consciousness that makes them wise,
The Good Supreme that they and we anthem ;
Transplanted we shall join the Parent Stem
From which we fell ; transfigured now we rise
In love, the very radiance of the skies,
In love which was before sin might intrude,
Which speaks on earth in each beatitude,
When sin's last wage is paid, which still will be
When time is rounded to an interlude,
And stellar space is a great inland sea,
In love, the heaven of the Deity.

THE END.

BRADBURY, AGNEW, & CO , PRINTERS, WHITEFRIARS

CPSIA information can be obtained
at www.ICGtesting.com
Printed in the USA
BVHW041934241120
594118BV00016B/305